PIANO • VOCAL • GUITAR

THE MARTY ROBBINS SONGBOOK

HAL•LEONARD®
CORPORATION

7777 W. BLUEMOUND RD. P.O. BOX 13819 MILWAUKEE, WI 53213

EL PASO

Words and Music by MARTY ROBBINS

Moderato

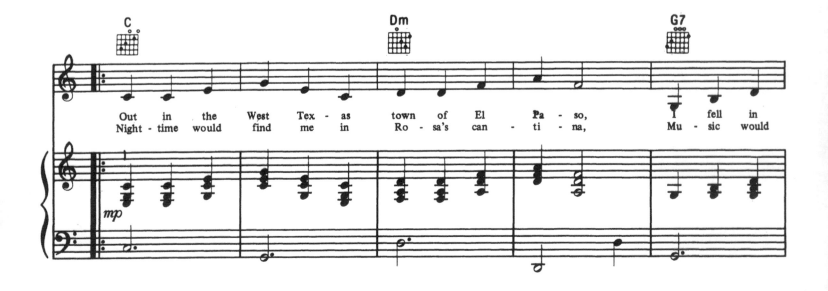

Out in the West Tex - as town of El Pa - so,   I fell in
Night - time would find me in Ro - sa's can - ti - na,   Mu - sic would

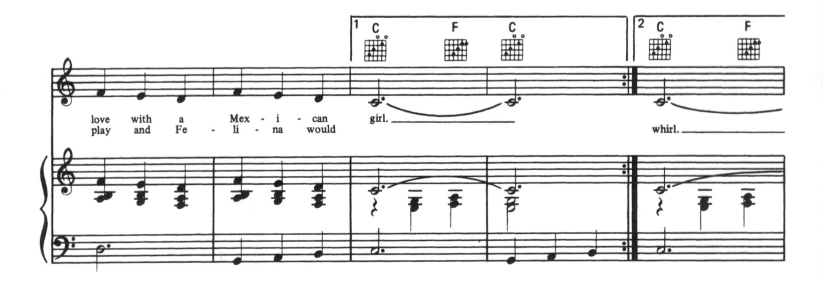

love with a Mex - i - can girl. _____
play and Fe - li - na would whirl. _____

4

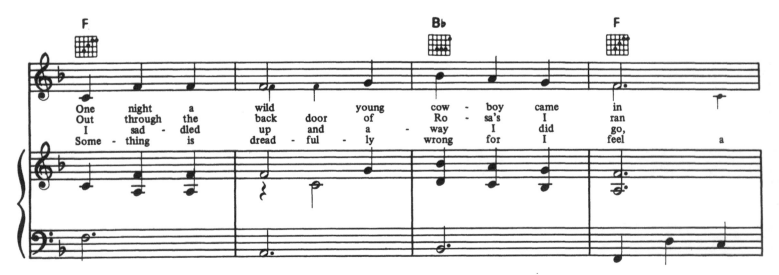

One   night   a   wild   young   cow - boy   came   in
Out   through   the   back   door   of   Ro - sa's   I   ran
I   sad - dled   up   and   a - way   I   did   go,
Some - thing   is   dread - ful - ly   wrong   for   I   feel   a

Wild   as   the   West   Tex - as   wind.
Out   where   the   hors - es   were   tied.
Rid - ing   a - lone   in   the   dark.
deep   burn - ing   pain   in   my   side.

Dash - ing   and   dar - ing,   a   drink   he   was   shar - ing,   with
I   caught   a   good   one,   it   looked   like   it   could   run,
May - be   to - mor - row   a   bul - let   will   find   me,   To
Though   I   am   try - ing   to   stay   in   the   sad - dle,

wick - ed   Fe   na,   the   girl   that   I   loved.
Up   on   its   back   and   a - way   I   did   ride.
night   noth - ing's   worse   than   this   pain   in   my   heart.
I'm   get - ting   wear - y   un - a - ble   to   ride.

PADRE

Original French lyrics by JACQUES LARUE
Music by ALAIN ROMANS
English Lyrics by PAUL FRANCIS WEBSTER

SINGING THE BLUES

Words and Music by MELVIN ENDSLEY

Well I nev-er felt more like sing-ing the blues___ 'cause I nev-er thought___ that I'd ev-er lose___ your love, Dear Why'd you do me this way?_____ Well, I nev-er felt more like

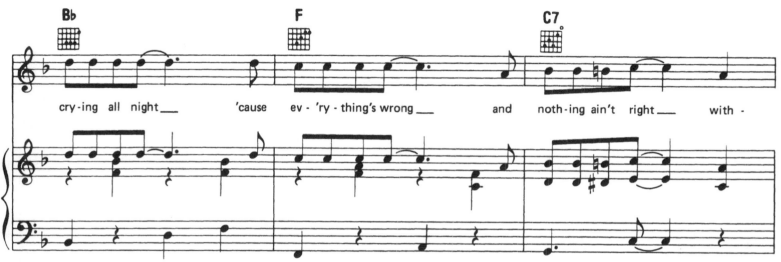

cry-ing all night ___ 'cause ev-'ry-thing's wrong ___ and noth-ing ain't right ___ with-

out you You got me sing-ing the blues _____ The

moon and stars no long-er shine, the dream is gone I

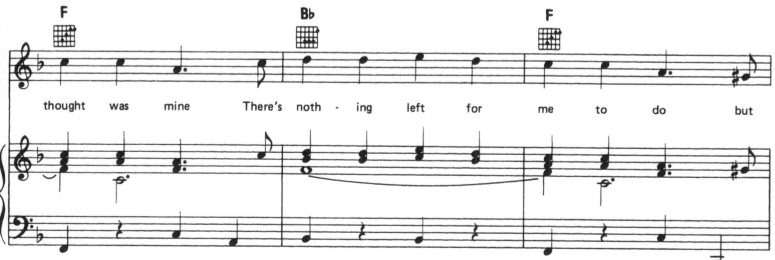

thought was mine There's noth-ing left for me to do but

A WHITE SPORT COAT

Words and Music by MARTY ROBBINS

DEVIL WOMAN

Words and Music by MARTY ROBBINS

2. Mary is waiting and weeping alone in our shack by the sea,
Even after I hurt her, Mary's still in love with me,
Devil woman, it's over, trapped no more by your charms,
I don't want to stay, I want to get away, woman, let go of my arms.

3. Devil woman, you're evil like the dark corral reef,
Like the winds that bring high tides, you bring sorrow and grief,
You made me ashamed to face Mary, barely had the strength to tell,
Skies are not so black, Mary took me back, Mary has broken your spell.

4. Running alone by the seashore, running as fast as I can.
Even the sea gulls are happy, glad I'm coming home again,
Never again will I ever cause another tear to fall.
Down the beach I see what belongs to me, the one I want most of all.

Last Chorus
Devil woman, devil woman, don't follow me,
Devil woman, let me be, just leave me alone, I want to go home.

AMONG MY SOUVENIRS

Words by EDGAR LESLIE
Music by HORATIO NICHOLLS

Slowly, With Expression

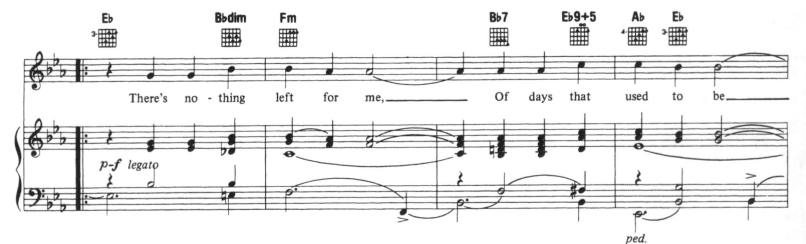

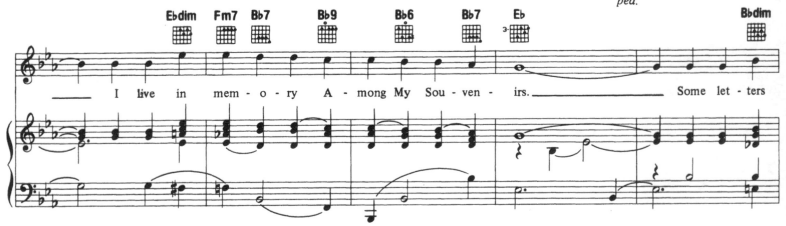

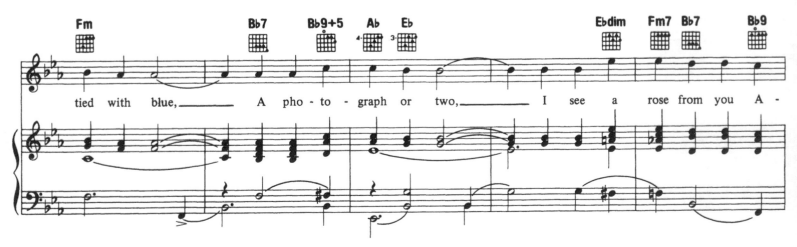

CAMELIA

Words and Music by MARTY ROBBINS

From where I stand I can see all the lights of the
If there was one ounce of man left in me, I'd ac-

cit - y, _____ For one man to
cuse her, _____ What's left of a

love _____ one wom-an so much, it's a pit-y. _____
man knows for cer-tain if I do, I'll love her. _____

From where I stand I can see the can-
It would-n't do____ to let her know

ti - na she goes to,____ Where she's not sup-
I know she's ly - in',____ Or that I'd been

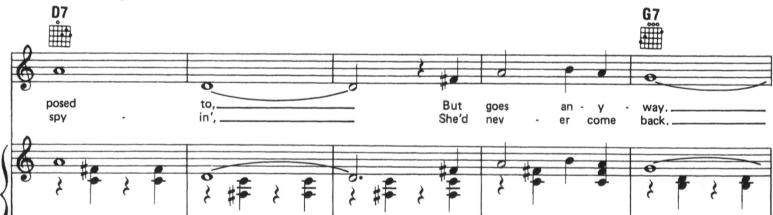

posed to,____ But goes an - y - way.____
spy - in',____ She'd nev - er come back.____

From where I stand I can
Ca - me - lia, I al - most de-

WHAT IF I SAID I LOVE YOU

Words and Music by CHARLIE BLACK
and TOMMY ROCCO

BEGGING TO YOU

Words and Music by MARTY ROBBINS

You don't want my lov-ing, _____ but you let me stay 'round. _____ I guess just to

walk on, _____ so you don't touch the ground. _____ To you it don't

mat-ter _____ what you cause me to do, _____ as long as you

keep me _____ beg-ging to you. _____

HONKYTONK MAN

Easy Country Waltz

Words and Music by DEWAYNE BLACKWELL

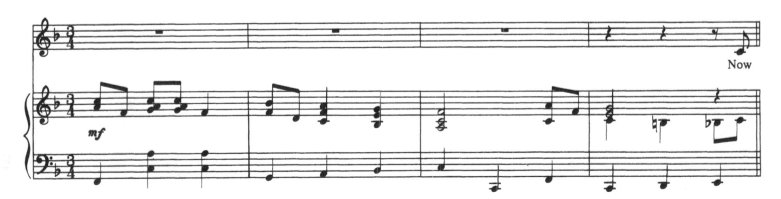

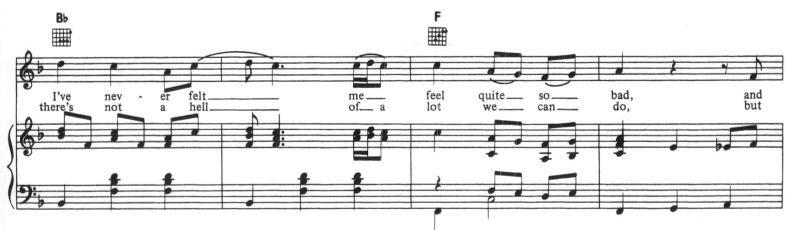

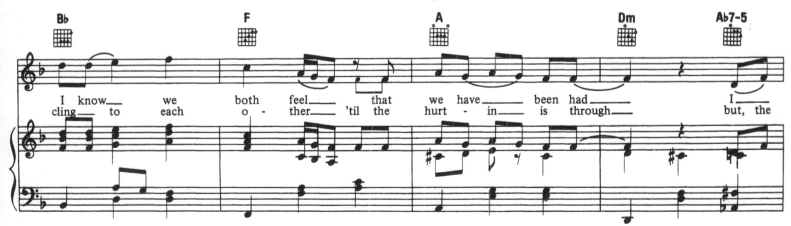

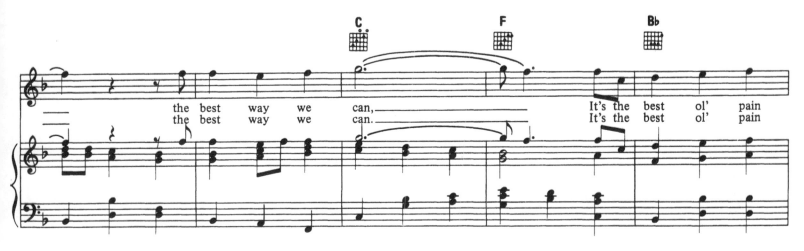

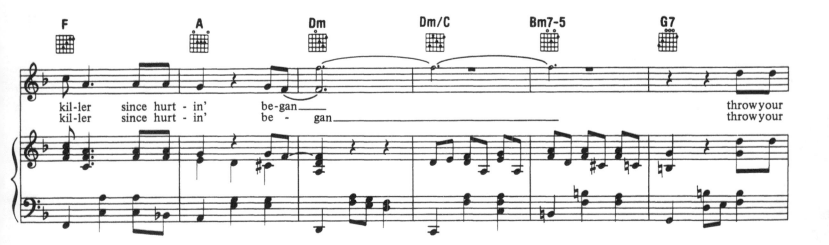

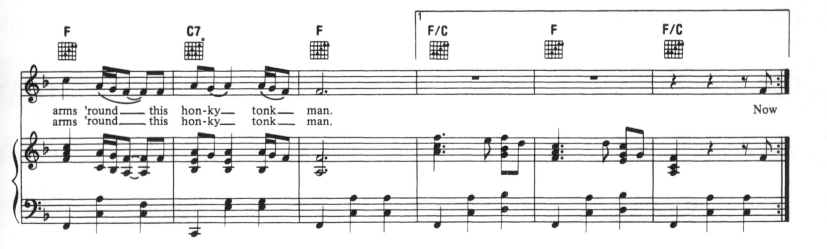

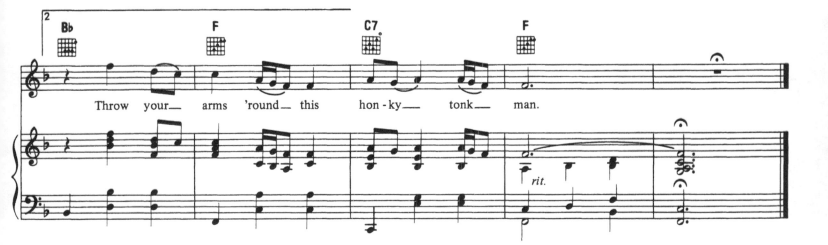

TONIGHT CARMEN

Words and Music by MARTY ROBBINS

DON'T WORRY

Words and Music by MARTY ROBBINS

BIG IRON

Words and Music by MARTY ROBBINS

3. Wasn't long before the story was relayed to Texas Red,
   But the outlaw didn't worry, men that tried before were dead,
   Twenty men had tried to take him, twenty men had made the slip,
   Twenty one would be the ranger with the Big Iron on his hip, Big Iron on his hip.
   The morning passed so quickly it was time for them to meet,
   It was twenty past eleven when they walked out in the street,
   Folks were watching from the windows, ev-'rybody held their breath,
   They knew this handsome ranger was about to meet his death, About to meet his death.

4. There was forty feet between them when they stopped to make their play,
   And the swiftness of the ranger is still talked about today.
   Texas Red had not cleared leather for a bullet fairly ripped.
   And the ranger's aim was deadly with the Big Iron on his hip, Big Iron on his hip.
   It was over in a moment and the folks had gathered 'round,
   There before them lay the body of the out-law on the ground.
   Oh he might have went on living but he made a fatal slip
   When he tried to match the ranger with the Big Iron on his hip, Big Iron on his hip.

THE COWBOY IN THE CONTINENTAL SUIT

With a beat

Words and Music by MARTY ROBBINS

1. He walked out in the a - re - na, all dressed up to the
   snick - ered at the way he dressed, but he nev - er said a

brim, He said he just came down from a place called High - land
word, He walked on by the rest of us as if he had - n't

Rim; Well, he said he came to ride the horse, the one they called "The
heard; A thou - sand bucks went to the man that could ride this wild cay -

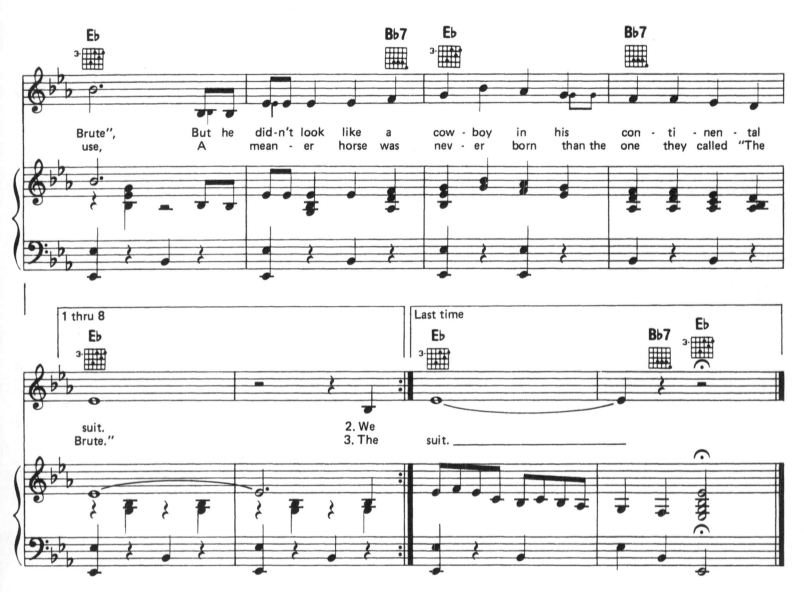

3. The horse that he was looking for was in chute number eight,
   He walked up very slowly, put his hand upon the gate;
   We knew he was a thoroughbred when he pulled a sack of Dukes,
   From the inside pocket of his continental suit.

4. He rolled himself a Quirley and he lit it standing there,
   He blew himself a smoke ring and he watched it disappear;
   We thought he must be crazy when he opened up the gate,
   Standing just inside was fifteen hundred pounds of hate.

5. The buckskin tried to run him down, but the stranger was too quick,
   He stepped aside and threw his arms around the horse's neck;
   He pulled himself upon the back of the horse they called "The Brute,"
   And sat like he was born there in his continental suit.

6. The Brute's hind end was in the air, his front end on the ground,
   A-kickin' and a-squeelin', trying to shake the stranger down;
   But the stranger didn't give an inch, he came to ride The Brute,
   And he came to ride the buckskin in a continental suit.

7. I turned around to look at Jim and he was watching me,
   He said, "I don't believe the crazy things I think I see;
   But I think I see the outlaw, the one they call "The Brute,"
   Ridden by a cowboy in a continental suit."

8. The Brute came to a standstill, ashamed that he'd been rode,
   By a city cowboy in some continental suit;
   The stranger took his money, we don't know where he went,
   We don't know where he came from, and we haven't seen him since.

9. The moral of this story, never judge by what they wear,
   Underneath some ragged clothes could be a millionaire;
   So everybody, listen, don't be fooled by this galoot,
   The sure enough bronc-buster in the continental suit.

IT'S YOUR WORLD

Words and Music by MARTY ROBBINS

GIRL FROM SPANISH TOWN

Moderately, with a Latin feeling

Words and Music by MARTY ROBBINS